HUMAN RESOURCE/
LABOR RELATIONS

HUMAN RESOURCE/ LABOR RELATIONS

A PRIMER

JAMES H. HOPKINS JD SPHR

iUniverse, Inc.
New York Lincoln Shanghai

Human Resource/Labor Relations

A Primer

Copyright © 2006 by James H Hopkins

iUniverse books may be ordered through booksellers or by contacting:

iUniverse
2021 Pine Lake Road, Suite 100
Lincoln, NE 68512
www.iuniverse.com
1-800-Authors (1-800-288-4677)

ISBN-13: 978-0-595-38756-4 (pbk)
ISBN-13: 978-0-595-83139-5 (ebk)
ISBN-10: 0-595-38756-X (pbk)
ISBN-10: 0-595-83139-7 (ebk)

Printed in the United States of America

This book is dedicated to my dear Mother whose love of books was unsurpassed and my dear Wife without whose support it would never have happened.

TABLE OF CONTENTS

INTRODUCTION.. 1

STAFFING.. 2

Independent Contractor or Employee 2

Position Descriptions...3

Employment Applications 3

POSTER REQUIREMENTS.. 5

EMPLOYEE HANDBOOK/COMPANY POLICIES 5

EMPLOYMENT-AT-WILL.. 6

General Rule 6

Exceptions...6

Breach of an Employment Contract 6

Opposition to Illegal Actions... 7

Contradiction of Employee Handbook.............................. 7

Violation of Statutes 8

FEDERAL STATUTES GOVERNING THE EMPLOYEE/
EMPLOYER RELATIONSHIP... 8

EMPLOYEE RETIREMENT INCOME SECURITY ACT (ERISA)... 9

NATIONAL LABOR RELATIONS ACT (NLRA)........................ 10

Employee Relations 10

Compensation 11

Promotions... 12

Job Security 13

Employer Awareness 14

Union Organizing 14

Negotiating a Collective Bargaining Agreement (CBA) 20

Good Faith Bargaining 20

Subjects of Bargaining (Generally) 20

Mandatory..21

Permissive..21

Illegal subject of bargaining 21

The Process Begins 22

Preparation 22

Who 22

What 23

Establish Goals.. 23

Evaluate Costs.. 23

Evaluate Effects of Reaching an Impasse........... 24

When 24

Why 25

The Initial Negotiation Meeting 25

Recess 26

Follow Up Meetings 26

FEDERAL FAIR LABOR STANDARDS ACT (FLSA) 27

Compensatory Time Off in Lieu of Payment.........................27

Exemptions 28

Executive 28

Administrative 29

Professional 29

Computer Employee 30

Outside Sales 31

Highly Compensated Employee 31

Applying the Exemption Test..31

Time Cards 32

Equal Pay for Equal Work 32

AGE DISCRIMINATION IN EMPLOYMENT (ADEA) 34

OCCUPATIONAL SAFETY AND HEALTH (OSHA).................. 34

CONSOLIDATED OMNIBUS BUDGET RECONCILIATION
ACT (COBRA)... 35

EMPLOYEE POLYGRAPH PROTECTION 36

WORKERS' ADJUSTMENT AND RETRAINING
NOTIFICATION (WARN) 36

FAMILY MEDICAL LEAVE ACT (FMLA) 38

DRUG FREE WORKPLACE ACT OF 1988 39

CIVIL RIGHTS 39

EQUAL EMPLOYMENT OPPORTUNITIES (EEO) 40

Religion..40

Race/Color 40

National Origin...41

Sex 41

EQUAL OPPORTUNITIES FOR INDIVIDUALS WITH
DISABILITIES ACT, AKA THE AMERICAN DISABILITIES
ACT (ADA) 42

EVALUATING PERFORMANCE... 43

EMPLOYEE DISCIPLINE 44

TERMINATION 45

RECORD KEEPING REQUIREMENTS 45

CONCLUSION 46

APPENDIX A—POSITION DESCRIPTION 47

APPENDIX B—EMPLOYMENT APPLICATION 48

APPENDIX C—POSTER REQUIREMENTS 51

APPENDIX D—COMPANY POLICIES 54

APPENDIX E—FEDERAL STATUTES 59

APPENDIX F—PERFORMANCE EVALUATION 62

APPENDIX G—GUIDELINE TO EMPLOYEE SEPARATION ... 65

INTRODUCTION

The fastest growing segment of the U.S. economy seems to be businesses with fewer than 100 employees. This segment's growth, coupled with the trend in the United States toward decentralization or flattening of the management of organizations of all sizes, is pushing more of the responsibility for decisions affecting employee relations down the organizational chart. There are those that believe this is where management of Human Resources belongs.[1] Employers are required to make faster decisions and provide rapid turnaround of information regarding employees. Information will come from the many stakeholders in the organization, such as customers, employees, unions and governmental agencies, all this requiring employers to collect and distill the salient points quickly in order to reinforce employee behavior. Employers must also provide employees with the proper information required of them to accomplish their assigned tasks. Today's employer is therefore required to be knowledgeable of the laws that affect human resource and/or labor management regardless of the employer's degree of experience in human resource matters. This knowledge forms the structure that employers must operate within when dealing with their employees.

This primer is designed to assist employers in fulfilling this ever-expanding role. It is not intended to make its readers human resource management experts or employment lawyers, but should only be viewed as a supplement to those resources, as this is an ever changing area of the law. Employers should constantly update themselves through their professional advisors. Some may view these laws as unnecessary and an impediment to the success of an organization, however, until the laws are changed, they remain part of the employer/employee landscape. Employers who ignore the laws when dealing with their employees can find themselves facing time-consuming and expensive problems. Every employer must understand that compliance with these laws is every bit as critical to the success of an enterprise as raising capital, creating a viable product, or marketing.

---

1   Human Resource Forecast The Anderson School at UCLA (1996). The World is Flat Thomas L. Freidman (2005)

Hopefully, this primer will minimize the employer's exposure to problems and, in a small way, contribute to the success of the organization.

STAFFING

Obtaining the right individuals, for the right job, at the right time is one of the most important parts of human resource management. Before the search begins, the employer must decide whether the individual to be hired will be classified as an independent contractor or an employee of the organization. After that decision is made, the employer should create a position description for the opening. Finally, the employer should obtain an employment application from potential candidates. These initial steps will require an investment of time and resources from an employer, but the advance preparation will likely ensure a better result in the end.

Independent Contractor or Employee

When determining the issue of whether an individual is an independent contractor or an employee, the employer's right to control the manner and means by which an individual accomplishes the job will be addressed by a court, should a dispute arises as to an individual's work classification. In addition, the following factors will also be considered by the court: (1) skill required; (2) source of instruments and tools used on the job; (3) location of the work; (4) duration of the relationship; (5) whether the employer can assign additional tasks; (6) the extent the worker has discretion over when and how long to work; (7) the method of payment (i.e. lump sum or hourly); (8) the worker's role in hiring and paying assistants; (9) whether the work is part of the employer's regular business; (10) whether the employer is a business; (11) the handling of employee benefits; and (12) the tax treatment of the hired party.[2] Each of these factors will be given equal weight in determining the worker's classification as an employee or an independent contractor.

---

2   *Nationwide Mutual Ins. Co. v. Darden*, 503 U.S. 318 (1992)

Position Descriptions

A position description is an effective way to bring consistency and objectivity to the process of placing the right person in the right position. Outlined in Appendix A is the structure of a position description.

Once the position description is completed, obtaining qualified applicants can be done in many ways: (1) help-wanted advertisements; (2) professional employment recruiters; (3) referrals from existing employees; (4) referrals from the community at large; and (5) Internet postings.

The skill level required for the job to be filled will generally dictate which recruiting resource is used. Regardless of the source used to obtain applicants, the employer must seek a cross-section of applicants without regard for race, sex, etc., to comply with the discrimination laws.

Employment Applications

When it becomes necessary for an employer to hire a new employee, each applicant should be required to complete an employment application. Doing so will serve multiple purposes: (1) establish a record of who applies for position; (2) serve as a source of prospects for future hiring; and (3) assist in determining qualified candidates.

An employment application can take many forms. One over another is not necessarily good or bad. The main point is to ensure that the application does not seek discriminatory information regarding health, age, race, sex, etc; but, rather, but does seek the qualifications that the applicant has which will make him or her successful in the position for which they are applying. See Appendix B for an example of an employment application.

It is recommended that every applicant be required to complete and sign an employment application. In the event the employer only receives a resume from a prospective applicant, it is recommended that the applicant be required to sign and date the resume. Generally, when someone signs information, they understand that the accuracy of that information is important. In addition, any disciplinary action will be easier to defend, should it be discovered subsequent to hiring an individual, that she/he has been less than truthful on their resume and/or application.

The employer will use the application and an applicant interview to help reach a hiring decision. The employer will seek information which establishes the applicant's ability to perform the job, as identified in the position description. This needs to be done by seeking information that establishes the applicant's experience, education and skills. Information regarding age (other than if the applicant is over the age of 18), religion, national origin or other unlawful information must not be sought.[3] English only rules are also suspect.[4] English only rules in the workplace are permissible only when required by a business necessity.[5]

An employer cannot discriminate against an employee or prospective employee based on an individual's handicap. When an individual can perform the essential functions of the job, when given reasonable accommodations, they must be considered for the job.

References should be checked on applicants considered for hire. The employer will likely discover that previous employers will generally only verify information provided by the applicant; such as name, job title and last date worked. It is becoming an increased practice of former employers to request a release from their former employee prior to providing information. A sample of the type of document a prospective employee may be asked to sign in order to obtain information from previous employers is as follows:

> *The undersigned hereby authorizes (previous employer #1), previous employer #2) and (previous employer #3) to provide (prospective employer) to whom I am applying for employment, complete information regarding my employment. With each former employer, I*

---

3   This could also apply to height and weight inquiries; 29 C.F.R. §1606.6.

4   29 C.F.R. § 1606.7.

5   *Long v. First Union Corp. of Va.*, 894 F. Supp. 933 (E.D. Va. 1995).

hereby waive and hold harmless each for the information provided to
<u>*(prospective employer)*</u>.

_____*[applicant's signature]*

It is also recommended that an employer not provide information on any
of her/his former employees without a similar release.

POSTER REQUIREMENTS

Every employer is required to post certain notices in a conspicuous
place where they can be read by all employees. These notices outline the
employee's options under various statutes. These statutes will be discussed
in more detail later. A summary of the notices required by various governmental agencies and information on how to obtain them is outlined
in Appendix C.

EMPLOYEE HANDBOOK/COMPANY POLICIES

It is generally recommended that every employer develop an employee
handbook. The reason for developing policies and setting them out in
an employee handbook is twofold: (1) they will create an atmosphere of
fairness and consistency with regard to treatment of employees; and (2)
they will create an atmosphere in which employees understand what is
expected by the employer.

Some may recommend against developing an employee handbook because
failure to follow it can be the basis for a wrongful termination lawsuit in
some states.[6] For the most part, the improved employee relations derived
from the consistency and communicated expectations outweigh the risk,
although the risks can be minimized by placing a disclaimer in the Policy
Manual.[7]

---

6   *Teamsters v. American Collord Co.*, 4 F.3d 631 (8th Cir. 1993)

7   *Coatney v. Enterprise Rent-a-Car*, 897 F.Supp. 1205 (WD Ark. 1995)

A sample disclaimer would be:

> *This employee handbook has been written as a guideline and is not intended to form the basis of a contract between the employer and any employee. In addition, the policies contained herein can be changed at the sole discretion of the employer.*

The employee handbook should expressly state that it does not establish an employment contract, nor alter the employment-at-will status of any employee, and that it may be modified unilaterally and without notice to employee prior to any change by the employer.

Examples of areas that may be covered in an employee handbook are outlined in Appendix D.

EMPLOYMENT-AT-WILL

General Rule

An employer may terminate an employee for a good reason, a poor reason, or no reason at all.[8]

Exceptions

As with all rules, employment-at-will has its exceptions, which have been developed on a state-by-state basis over time.

• Breach of an Employment Contract

An employer is prohibited from terminating an employee when there is an employment contract for a specified period of time, except by the terms of the contract. Such a contract generally is required to be in writing and signed by both parties. However, state courts are becoming more sensitive to implied contracts and are looking at the totality of circumstances

---

8   *Adair v. U.S.*, 208 U.S. 161 (1908).

surrounding the employer-employee relationship.[9] Courts will generally require the employer give additional consideration beyond that which would be considered normal for hiring into the new position before finding an implied contract.[10] This could range from resigning a position in which long-term employment was guaranteed,[11] relying on the assurances of the new employer that the new position was long-term,[12] relocating a long distance with the assurance that employment would be for a specified time,[13] or possibly an offer letter in which compensation for the position is specified in terms of an annual salary, or some other similar term.[14]

• *Opposition to Illegal Actions*

Another exception to the general rule is that an employer cannot terminate an employee for opposing any illegal actions or unlawful procedures.[15] This could take the form of opposing improper filing of insurance claims, bringing to light violations of environmental laws, and/or opposing improper filing state unemployment or state worker's compensation claims.

• *Contradiction of Employee Handbook*

States will also require an employer to follow procedures set forth in any employee handbook. The rule is when an employer establishes terms and conditions for employment in an employee handbook, the employer is obligated to follow those procedures.[16]

9　*DePhilips v. Zolt Const. Co.*, 136 Wn.2d 26 (1998).

10　Ibid.

11　*F.S. Royster Guano Co. v. Hall*, 68 F.2d 533 (4th Cir. 1934).

12　*Tousant v. Blue Cross & Blue Shield*, 408 Mich. 579 (1980).

13　Ibid.

14　*Havens v. C&O Plastics*, 68 Wn. App. 159 (1992).

15　*Thompson v. St. Regis Paper Co.*, 102 Wn.2d 219 (1984).

16　*Kearney v. KXLF Communications, Inc.*, 869 P.2d 772 (1994).

• *Violation of Statutes*

The final, and perhaps most extensive, exception to the general employ-ment-at-will rule are the various statutes passed by Congress and the vari-ous state legislatures. There are approximately fifteen (15) federal statutes with hundreds of subsections which have an effect upon the employer-employee relationship. The significant federal statutes are outlined in Appendix E. No employee can be terminated in violation of any of these statutes. The federal statutes cover a wide range of topics. In addition, each state has numerous statutes with which an employer must also com-ply. The state statutes will cover a wide variety of areas such as discrimina-tion, wages, benefit plans, hours worked, and so on. Any employer with employees in a given state must be familiar with their state's employment laws.

When an employee is terminated in violation of one of the exceptions dis-cussed, that employee may have a case for wrongful termination, in addi-tion to any cause of action authorized by a statute. An employer should always keep the exceptions to the employment-at-will rule in mind when considering termination of an employee.

FEDERAL STATUTES GOVERNING THE EMPLOYEE/EMPLOYER RELATIONSHIP

The federal statutes only apply to employers engaged in interstate com-merce and who have the requisite number of employees. Interstate com-merce has been defined as sale of goods or services across a state bor-der.[17] See Appendix E for a list of federal statutes affecting the employer/employee relationship.

---

17   *Carter v. Carter Coal Co.*, 298 U.S. 238 (1935).

EMPLOYEE RETIREMENT INCOME SECURITY ACT (ERISA)

Employers recognize that the Employee Retirement Income Security Act (ERISA)[18] applies to pension/retirement plans, but ERISA goes beyond these plans to include "employee benefit" plans established or maintained by an employer.[19]

An employer cannot discharge, discipline, or discriminate against an individual who takes advantage of any benefits provided by an employer-sponsored employee benefit plan,[20] nor can an employer deny an employee access to these benefits, such as terminating an employee in retaliation for using accrued sick leave days.[21]

ERISA defines an employee as anyone who has a reasonable expectation of receiving a benefit, has relied upon that expectation to continue working, and lacks "economic bargaining" power to obtain by contract non-forfeitable rights.[22]

This goes beyond the traditional right-to-control test used to determine whether an individual is an independent contractor or an employee.[23] (A discussion of the right-to-control test is found on page 2).

---

18   29 U.S.C. 1001 et seq. (ERISA).

19   29 U.S.C. 1002(1)

20   29 U.S.C. 1140

21   *Kembro v. Atlantic Richfield Co.*, 889 F.2d 869 (9th Cir. 1989).

22   *Dardin v. Nationwide Insurance Co.*, 796 F.2d 701 (4th Cir. 1986).

23   *Nationwide Mutual Insurance v. Darden, supra,* Note 2.

NATIONAL LABOR RELATIONS ACT (NLRA)

Employee Relations

The possibility of a union attempting to organize a company's employees is a continuing concern for every employer operating in a non-union environment. Union elections are seldom won or lost during the time period between an election being ordered and an election being held—the outcome is determined by an employer's overall employee relations climate.

This section reviews why unions desire to organize and represent employees, why employees feel a need to have the support of a union, and what practices an employer can follow to create a positive climate to minimize the possibility of employees seeking unionization. Also outlined is the organizational drive; including preliminary signs, procedures for a determination election, and what an employer can and cannot do during the campaign prior to election.

Many employers may feel secure that their employees would never approach a union to request assistance in organizing fellow workers. Employers are generally shocked to find that union organizing efforts are generally inside jobs, meaning they are initiated by the employer's own employees. The union will become an enthusiastic participant in coordinating and financing the organizing effort when approached by an employer's own employees.

Unions sometimes target an industry and/or a particular company for organization. A non-union company in a heavily unionized geographic area or a specific industry may become a target. Certain industries, such as the many service industries, are attracting increased organizing activity.

The union philosophy is clear: the rank and file worker needs the protection of a Collective Bargaining Agreement (CBA). Employers who ignore the needs of their employees will undoubtedly find unions can and do provide a countervailing power structure for disenchanted workers.

The needs of individuals cannot be conveniently categorized and/or satisfied. Some individuals enjoy hard work, accept reasonable pay and expect a tyrannical employer. Others want little work, high pay and no supervision. Fortunately, in most companies, employees are reasonably satisfied with their jobs, pay and supervision. If the reasonably satisfactory conditions deteriorate, workers can withdraw and quit creating costly turnover, or they can stay and attempt to change the environment. One way to do so is to turn to a union. It is important for an employer to remember that what seems fair and reasonable to the employer may seem arbitrary and even ridiculous to the employee.

Some main areas of dissatisfaction that cause employees to support a union are: inequitable pay, favoritism by employers, poor supervision as defined by the employees, lack of appreciation, no outlet for complaints or suggestions, job insecurity, and we (the workers) versus they (the employer) mentality. Employers who fail to address these concerns are vulnerable to union organizing and/or high employee turnover.

An employer who feels it is in its best interest to remain non-union can create an employee relations climate that will help to minimize the prospect of unionization. Books have been written and seminars presented with methods to follow in an effort to remain non-union. The main areas that are common to all who advocate how to remain non-union are compensation, policies and practices, and employer awareness.

Compensation

An employer who holds wages and benefits below what the competition is paying may well find itself dealing with a union. Rates of pay and the total benefit package must fairly and competitively reflect the marketplace for the type of employee and employer needs. This external equity is not difficult to identify. Surveys of local, regional, or national wage rates can be used depending on the geographic region the employer must look to find qualified employees. Key or benchmark jobs can be utilized to provide an adequate comparison of jobs across industry lines and geographic regions. Traditionally, methods of giving increases have been automatic increases to a competitive job rate and merit increases. Increasingly, however, pay increases are being tied to some measure of productivity. The method used may depend upon the industry and/or the job. Basing increases on anything other than objective criteria such as productivity, performance, or the like, must not find its way into a compensation program or favoritism claims may be alleged. An employer must keep abreast of benefit improvements utilized by other in the industry. Employees may or may not be interested in some programs but it is better for the employer to determine what works for its employees than have a union assist in such a determination. An employer must stay in touch with the thinking of its employees regarding what programs are preferred.

Perceived internal equity problems are nearly impossible to eliminate. Virtually every employee can name at least one other employee who is perceived to contribute less and make more. But the employer should strive to maintain internal equity among its various positions. Whether by ranking positions, by point/factoring positions, or by a more sophisticated job evaluation system, the employer should be able to explain why certain jobs pay more than others. Job titles can also cause perceived inequity. For example, if a technician signs a piece of correspondence as administrator, other employees may feel that an under-the-table promotion has occurred.

Policies forbidding employees from talking with each other regarding their wages has been determined to be a violation of the NLRA, regardless of whether the employer is unionized or non-union.[24]

Employers must be aware of the external environment and provide competitive wages and benefits while striving to minimize internal problems, realizing that total elimination of perceived internal inequity is nearly impossible, but still is a worthwhile goal.

Promotions

Contrary to what most employers believe, many employees susceptible to unionization have no lofty ambition for promotion, but just wish to be treated fairly. When an employee does desire promotional opportuni-

---

24   *NLRB v. Main Street Terrace Care Center*, 218 F.3rd 531 (6th Cir. 2000)

ties, such opportunities must be made available in a fair and equitable manner. The safest method to accomplish this is to use straight seniority as the basis for making promotional decisions. One danger of a seniority system of promotion is that it may allow employees to stay with the company and move up whether or not they are the best performers. A formal system for promotion will go a long way to negate the "who you know" syndrome that can become part of an employer's culture. The best method to provide an equitable promotion path is by notifying employees of available openings, setting forth the defined minimum qualifications and performance levels, and then evaluating the seniority of the applicants who meet the criteria.

When individuals are passed over for promotion it hurts, but having no outlet for a complaint without fear of reprisal will just compound the hurt and create additional problems. Employers must encourage employees to bring concerns to the attention of someone who has the authority to respond, whether a formal grievance system, an open-door policy, or an ombudsmen is in place. All these methods can be effective if employees can use them, get results, and not fear retaliation. An open door policy, or any other method, will only be successful if management gets up from behind their desks and go through the open door to where the employees work, showing that management is approachable.

Job Security

The final area of employee concern often neglected by employers is the issue of job security. When times are good, no one thinks about being laid off. But as stories of impending cutbacks hit the six o'clock news, workers become fearful of losing their jobs. These concerns effect productivity. An employer should develop policies and procedure for staff reductions when business is good and such issues are the furthest thing from anyone's mind. Most staff reduction plans follow seniority or performance or a combination of both to determine who is to be involved in the reduction in force. The plan should be the basis of responding to employees when questions concerning layoffs arise.

Employer Awareness

Employers must take time to learn the concerns of their employees; all are not motivated by the same needs and desires. Awareness is critical in creating a healthy, competitive work environment.

Employers who pay little or no attention to the ideas, suggestions and general concerns of their workers will have a difficult time refuting the union's argument that the employees need to belong to a union. Some traditional methods of participation are the question box, suggestion systems, attitude surveys, general communication meetings or some form of electronic feedback. Many employers set up such systems, but workers must see results from their input if they are to feel that whatever system is utilized is effective. E-mail is an effective way of communicating with employees, but as in all communication, it must be two-way to be effective.

Union Organizing

Even when an employer follows sound employment practices, it may be faced with a campaign to organize a union.

A union representative election is not, for the most part, won or lost at the ballot box on election day, but rather, by a constant vigilance, or lack thereof, each and every day. Employers must develop credibility with their employees so every employee will feel comfortable in voicing their concerns. In this way, any union activity should be brought to the employer's attention before it has developed into a full-fledged campaign. The employer's responsibility is to see that management is trained for and has developed good human relations skills.

An employer may also be alerted to possible union activities by individuals handing out handbills or leaflets to employees as they enter or leave the premises, handbills/leaflets appearing on bulletin boards or cafeteria tables and increased E-mail activity discussing company weaknesses and/or union's strength.

Another obvious sign that a union is attempting to organize a workforce is when authorization cards are circulated among employees. An authorization card is generally a 3" x 5" card that may request an election for a particular union,[25] or it may be a union membership card,[26] or it may be a dues check-off authorization.[27] If authorization cards are used, the union will be required to obtain members if it wins the election; however, employees who sign either membership cards or check-off authorizations are automatically members of the union if the union is successful in an election.

Still another way for an employer to become aware that a union is attempting to organize its workforce is if employees are acting out of the ordinary. Some signs to watch for are employees meeting in unusual groupings and/or employees discontinuing conversation when management approaches. These actions are at best ambiguous and should not be taken automatically as a sign of union activity, after all, the employees could be planning a manager's surprise birthday party.

Finally, union officials may contact the employer directly.

The majority of employees in any appropriate bargaining unit may choose a union to represent them in dealings with their employer. Through the NLRA[28], Congress assigned the National Labor Relations Board (NLRB)[29] broad discretion in determining the appropriate bargaining unit for collective bargaining purposes. The NLRB, for its part, has not established any hard and fast rules which would define such a unit, but

---

25   *NLRB v. Stow Mfg. Co.*, 217 F.2d 900 (2nd Cir. 1954) <u>cert. denied</u>, 348 U.S. 964 (1955).

26   *NLRB v. Federbush Co.*, 121 F.2d 954 (2nd Cir. 1941)

27   *Lebanon Steel Foundry v. NLRB*, 130 F.2d 404 (CA DC 1942).

28   29 U.S.C. § 141, *et seq.*

29   National Labor Relations Board, established by Congress with the National Labor Relations Act of 1935.

instead it applies certain tests to each petition submitted by employees, unions or companies. These tests identify:[30]

(1) extent and type of union organization currently in place among the employees;

(2) bargaining history in the industry, as well as with respect to the parties before the Board;

(3) similarity of duties, skills, interests, and working conditions of the employees;

(4) organizational structure of the company; and

(5) the desires of the employees

If a union or employees gather what is believed to be a sufficient number of authorization cards, they may petition the company directly for recognition. In the event an employer is asked to recognize a union, it has two choices: (1) if convinced the union represents a majority of the employees, the employer can voluntarily recognize the union; or (2) if there is a basis for a good faith doubt of the union's claim of majority status, the employer can petition the NLRB for a representation election. In the event an employer determines the union has the support of a majority of the employees but still refuses to bargain, the NLRB may issue a bargaining order without an election.[31] Employers should keep this in mind and not take a private poll of employees or review any authorization cards presented by the union. Before the NLRB will order an election, it must determine there is a substantial number of employees in the appropriate bargaining unit wishing to be represented by the union.[32] By rule, the NLRB has defined an appropriate number as thirty percent or more of the employees in the appropriate unit.[33] The biggest issue at this stage

---

30   *NLRB v. Hearst Publications, Inc.*, 322 U.S. 111 (1944).

31   *NLRB v. Gissel Packing Co.*, 395 U.S. 575 (1969); *Sullivan Electric Co.*, 199 NLRB 809 (1974).

32   29 U.S.C. § 159(c)(1)(A).

33   NLRB Rules and Regulations Series 8 as amended § 101.18(a).

will be identifying the appropriate unit. It is in the best interest of the employer wishing to remain non-union to have the appropriate unit to be larger and include as many pro-employer employees. The union will want just the opposite; the larger the appropriate unit, the more difficult to obtain the thirty percent show of interest required for an election. Remember, the employer is better off if the NLRB never directs an election to take place if remaining non-union is the goal.

When deciding whether to argue that a group of employees are in the bargaining unit it must be kept in mind that if a bargaining order is directed by the NLRB, all employees, pro-union and pro-employer, will be in the appropriate unit and will be part of the collective bargaining process.

When the NLRB directs an election, a simple majority of those eligible employees <u>actually voting</u>[34] is the requirement to have the union certified as the bargaining agent for all of the employees in the appropriate unit. To put this in perspective, if the appropriate unit consists of ten employees, four or more may petition for an election. If four vote in the election, three voting for the union will cause certification of the union as the bargaining agent for the ten employees in that appropriate unit. Obviously, it is in the employer's best interest to have all employees vote. The union will not be certified on the basis of a tie vote.[35]

During the organizing campaign, the employer may not restrain, coerce or interfere[36] with an employee's right[37] to join or refrain from joining or voting for a union.[38] An employer can speak out if opposed to having a union represent their employees. Every employer has the right to let the employees know of their opposition to the union,[39] but there can be

---

34   29 U.S.C. § 159(a), *RCA Mfg. Co.*, 2 NLRB 159 (1936).

35   *John W. Thomas Co.*, 111 NLRB 226 (1955).

36   29 U.S.C. § 158(a)(1).

37   Ibid.

38   29 U.S.C. § 157.

39   29 U.S.C. § 158(c).

neither direct nor indirect promise of benefits in return for an employee failing to support the union, nor threats of retaliation if an employee supports the union.[40]

During an organizing campaign: (1) employees may solicit their fellow employees for union support during their non-working, free time. This has been defined as lunch time, scheduled coffee breaks, time before or after the start of a regularly scheduled shift and even time standing in line to punch a time clock;[41] (2) employees may distribute union handbills or leaflets to other employees in non-working areas, but may be excluded from doing so in work areas.[42] Attempts made to keep employees from verbalizing their feelings regarding unions during work time when they are not otherwise restricted from visiting about other topics are prohibited;[43] (3) solicitation during work time can be prevented.[44] A solicitation policy that prohibits the solicitation of employees by non-employees on the premises should be developed. Non-employee union organizer can be prohibited from coming on to the premises to distribute union literature.[45] However, this can only be enforced when permission has been withheld for all non-employee solicitation. Generally, an exception to this rule is for solicitation by a charity, although if these are allowed quite broadly, a finding of discrimination against the union is quite probable.[46] A non-solicitation policy cannot be instituted at the outset of a union organizing campaign with any expectation of enforcement by the NLRB;[47] (4) employers may forbid the wearing of union

---

40   *NLRB v. Gissel Packing Co., supra.* footnote 35.

41   *Stoddard-Quirk Mfg. Co.*, 138 NLRB 615 (1962).

42   *F.W. Woolworth Co. v. NLRB*, 530 F.2d 1245 (2nd Cir. 1976) <u>cert. denied</u> 429 U.S. 1023 (1976).

43   *Marathon Le Tourneau Co., Longview Div. v. NLRB*, 699 F.2d 248 (5th Cir. 1983).

44   *Our Way, Inc.*, 268 NLRB 61 (1983).

45   *NLRB v. Babcock & Wilcox*, 351 U.S. 105 (1956).

46   *Hammary Mfg. Co., Div. of U.S. Industries, Inc.*, 265 NLRB 57 (1982) amending 258 NLRB 1319 (1981).

47   *NLRB v. Roney Plaza Apts.*, 597 F.2d 1046 (5th Cir. 1979).

buttons or insignias by its employees;[48] (5) once a union campaign gets under way, there can be no unilateral change to wages or benefits by the employer.[49] Although there seems to be no clear rule as to when the campaign begins, common sense would seem to dictate that it is when the employer becomes aware of the union's intent to organize the employees. It is doubtful this means that the union can notify an employer in an attempt to keep changes from being made with no actual intent to organize the workforce. The facts of each situation will be determinative. Once again, there are exceptions to this ban on changes, such as when the change was planned before the start of the campaign.[50] Before any changes are made, the circumstances should be carefully evaluated; (6) predictions as to the possible consequences should the employees support the union can be made, provided the predicted results are beyond the employer's control.[51] This means threats of plant closure or plant relocation due to the unionizing are prohibited.[52] Statements that the added financial burden, if any, could put the employer out of business, assuming there is a current financial hardship, are permissible;[53] (7) the benefits, if any, that employees currently have in a non-union company should also be discussed. After all, an employee may not realize the extent of their total benefit package. This awareness of benefits to employees is another part of a day-to-day employee relations program; (8) the employees' attention may be drawn to what the union's policies and practices are in dealing with members; and (9) neither side may make speeches to the employees during the 24-hour period just prior to the election.[54]

---

48   *Republic Aviation v. NLRB*, 324 U.S. 793 (1945).

49   *Red's Express*, 268 NLRB 1154 (1984).

50   Ibid.

51   *Patsy Bee, Inc. v. NLRB*, 654 F.2d 515 (8th Cir. 1981).

52   *Nebraska Bulls Transp. v. NLRB*, 608 F.2d 311 (8th Cir. 1979).

53   *Chripler Airtemp S.C., Inc.*, 224 NLRB 427 (1976).

54   *Peerless Plywood Co.*, 107 NLRB 427 (1953).

Negotiating a Collective Bargaining Agreement (CBA)

When an employer's employees are represented by a union, bargaining in good faith with the union's representative in an attempt to reach a CBA is required.[55] The union representing the employees is also obligated to bargain in good faith with the employer.[56]

Good Faith Bargaining

Good faith bargaining requires the employer and the union to meet with the honest intention of reaching agreement. Good faith bargaining does not require a CBA to be agreed upon. The NLRB and the courts will look to all the circumstances surrounding the negotiations to determine whether good faith bargaining has taken place.[57] An employer's obligation to bargain in good faith goes beyond just meeting at reasonable times with the union. The employer must provide information to the union as part of the duty to bargain in good faith, which includes all information that is relevant and needed by the union to fulfill its obligation to negotiate. Failure to furnish the required information will be considered by the NLRB and the courts as part of the totality of the circumstance surrounding negotiations when determining whether an employer is negotiating in good faith.[58]

If an employer claims an inability to pay as a basis for not agreeing to a wage and/or benefit proposal made by the union, the financial condition of the employer becomes relevant to the negotiations, and the employer must provide financial data on the company to the union.[59]

Subjects of Bargaining (Generally)

The subjects for negotiating a CBA generally fall into three areas: (1) mandatory; (2) permissive; and (3) illegal.

---

55   29 U.S.C. § 158(d).

56   Ibid.

57   *NLRB v. Fitzgerald Mills Corp.*, 313 F.2d 260 (5th Cir. 1963).

58   *K-Mart Corp. v. NLRB,* 626 F.2d 704 (9th Cir. 1980).

59   *NLRB v. Unoco Apparel, Inc.,* 508 F.2d 1368 (5th Cir. 1975).

Mandatory

Mandatory subjects of bargaining are: (1) "…rates of pay, wages, hours of employment, or other conditions of employment"[60] and (2) "…wages, hours and other terms and conditions of employment."[61]

Permissive

Permissive subjects of bargaining are those items that fall outside the mandatory framework.[62] The employer and union cannot reach an impasse over permissive subjects of bargaining.[63]

Illegal subject of bargaining

Illegal subjects of bargaining are any topics that by their very nature violate some rule of law, such as:

(1) Requiring union membership by an applicant prior to being considered for employment or hired for a position (i.e. "closed shop" requirement).[64] A union shop clause in a contract is permissible, but in "right to work" states,[65] such clauses cannot be enforced. In a union shop, membership is not required for hiring consideration, but is required at some point after being hired.

(2) A union giving hiring hall preferences to its membership and/or excluding non-union applicants.

---

60   29 U.S.C. 159(a).

61   29 U.S.C. 158(d).

62   *NLRB v. Wooster Div. Borg-Warner Corp.*, 356 U.S. 342, 2 Led 823, 78 § 718 (1958).

63   Ibid.

64   *Panello v. Mine Workers*, 88 F. Supp. 935 (D DC 1950).

65   "Right to work" states are: Alabama, Arizona, Arkansas, North Carolina, South Carolina, North Dakota, South Dakota, Florida, Georgia, Idaho, Iowa, Kansas, Louisiana, Mississippi, Nevada, Nebraska, Tennessee, Texas, Utah, Virginia and Wyoming

(3) The parties to a CBA agreeing not to handle goods of a third party, so called "hot cargo."[66]

The Process Begins

When negotiating a CBA, the negotiation process will generally follow a predictable pattern, regardless of who is taking part. The steps which make up the process are: (1) preparation; (2) initial meeting; (3) recess; and (4) follow up meeting(s).

Preparation

A thorough preparation is the key to successful negotiations. Until all parties have invested the time and effort in fully preparing themselves, face-to-face negotiations are not practical.

The first step in preparing for negotiations is to conduct objective fact-finding to determine the who, what, when and why of the negotiations.

<u>Who</u>: Those individuals on both sides of the negotiations who will be critical to reaching an agreement must be identified. While the personalities of the participants should not play a part, in reality, it is difficult to remove this aspect completely from the process. Therefore, it may be necessary to incorporate the participants' personalities into the fact-finding process.

A significant factor in the "who" stage is the employer's selection of the Negotiator. The selected individual should not be the most senior individual at the employer. This allows the Negotiator the flexibility to respond to proposals by stating that she/he "must talk with the boss" before responding. However, the Negotiator must be given significant authority to conduct negotiations or the company may be charged with failure to bargain in good faith.[67] The Negotiator should also have experience in negotiating collective bargaining agreements; this is more impor-

---

66   29 U.S.C. 159(e).

67   *Unbelievable, Inc. dba Frontier Hotel & Casino*, 318 NLRB 857, 150 LRRM 1065 (1995).

tant than having experience in any particular industry. Experience and knowledge of the process of collective bargaining gives the Negotiator the ability to evaluate the union's demands and the union's resolve on any particular issue. A miscalculation as to the union's or employer's position at any time during the process can give rise to disastrous consequences.

What: The negotiator must have a clear understanding of the employer's goals for the negotiations.

Establish Goals

The employer should establish the goals to be achieved during the collective bargaining process. The employer should identify those areas of the existing CBA which it feels have been the most troublesome. Each area should be prioritized; commencing with those areas where changes are most needed, to those areas where changes are desired but not necessary.

To assist in establishing these goals, the employer should review (1) the history of the CBA currently in effect; (2) each grievance filed by the union; and (3) the contract, article by article. This is done to determine if CBA language should be changed, or whether past practice and the CBA are not in synch. Past practices between the company and the union are part of the CBA[68] unless specifically negotiated out. This can cause many disputes and should be addressed. Arbitration decisions, if any, need to be reviewed as well. The history of the working relationship between the employer and the union should be considered and altered if necessary to achieve the desired results. The employer should survey all management personnel to determine which areas of the contract they may find troublesome. Generally, senior management will be concerned with the economics of the agreement, while first line supervisors will be concerned with work rules.

Evaluate Costs

A cost analysis of the current contract is a must. The cost analysis should review the cost of wages, benefits, work rules, and any other direct costs

---

68   Alpena Gen. Hospital, 50 LA 48 (1967).

or creators of inefficiencies in the work place. The time to commence the process of gathering this information is immediately after completion of the negotiations on the previous CBA. There should also be a cost analysis prepared as outlined above for competitors, both union and non-union.

There should be an evaluation of current levels of finished goods in inventory if the employer is in the manufacturing industry, as well as a complete sales projections for the term of the anticipated contract, specifically for the anticipated time during which negotiations will be taking place. This information will provide an evaluation of the effect the collective bargaining process will have on sales.

Evaluate Effects of Reaching an Impasse

An impasse during negotiations of a CBA is that point where further negotiations would not produce an agreement.[69] At this point, the employer can implement its last contract proposal presented to the union.[70]

Employers must determine the impact an impasse would have on business. An impasse could lead to a strike, the impact of which needs to be calculated well in advance of it occurring. In addition, a determination as to laws effecting the use of replacement workers must be made. An employer may choose to lock-out non-striking employees in the event of a strike. Any decision on this matter needs to be reviewed well in advance of any action being taken and should take into account the impact on sales, production, customer relations, and relationships with non-union employees, as well as the relationship with bargaining unit employees after a new CBA is reached. Another factor which should be considered is the fact that locked-out employees may be eligible for unemployment benefits, which may increase the employer's unemployment insurance rates in the future.

When: The time frame in which the negotiations must commence and/ or be completed should be specified. If no firm time frame applies, it is

---

69   *NLRB v. AMF Bowling Co.*, 63 F.3d 1293 (4th Cir. 1995).

70   *NLRB v. Plainville Ready Mix Concrete Co.*, 44 F.3d 1320 (6th Cir. 1995).

still a good idea to establish a time line to keep the process on track and moving forward at a reasonable pace.

Why: Both the desired results and the justification of the results should be well-known and clearly identified. The ultimate purpose of the negotiations should not be to crush the other side, but to accomplish an economic result.

By answering these questions, the employer will determine the goals for the negotiations in a rational, logical manner.

While establishing goals, the minimal acceptable position and a maximum expected position should be set by the employer. The union will be contemplating its range as well. Where these ranges overlap will determine the settlement range (see illustration).

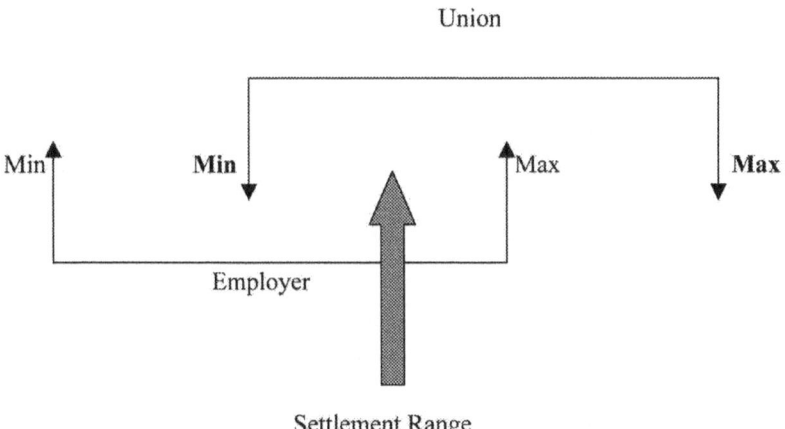

The Initial Negotiation Meeting

When the preparation process is complete, it will be time to commence the actual negotiations. During the initial meeting, the union will generally put its proposal on the table and make a general statement as to why they believe their position is just. The employer will verify the information developed during the preparation phase.

The parties should establish a civil working environment with the under-standing that the best end result may not make the employer or the union happy, but is considered to be as fair as possible to all involved. If either negotiator appears completely inflexible during the first meeting, it may signal the collapse of the negotiations and ensure a charge of bad faith bargaining.

The negotiators should determine where and when future meetings will be held.

By listening carefully and with thorough preparation, the employer will identify early those items the union deems important.

Recess

There should be a recess after the initial meeting to evaluate the informa-tion received as well as the employer's position. Such a recess may range from a few minutes to a few days. The time frame set out in the prepara-tion phase may dictate how short a recess should be. Another factor in determining the length of the recess is how long it will take for both sides to digest the information provided and to evaluate this information in conjunction with the information set forth in the preparation phase.

During this time, the settlement range may be narrowed based upon the give and take explored during the initial meeting.

Follow Up Meetings

Depending upon the strengths and/or weakness of the employer and union, an overall bargaining strategy and bargaining style will begin to emerge. This strategy and style will set the tone for any future meetings.

The strategy may be to settle early or taking a tougher position in an attempt to move higher in the settlement range. Again, keep in mind the goals first established and continue working on separating the people from the issues.

Negotiating styles will depend upon the relationship negotiators have established. The style may be affected by prior negotiations.

In the final analysis, a good negotiator will focus on being positive during the negotiations, being a good listener, and at all times being considerate of the individuals with whom she/he is negotiating.

Using objective criteria during negotiations and keeping options open to create mutual gain will generally lead to a satisfactory result.

FEDERAL FAIR LABOR STANDARDS ACT (FLSA)

Many employers struggle with the question of when and to who is overtime pay required and whether it must be paid or can be taken as compensatory time.

The law which primarily governs the issue of overtime compensation is the FLSA,[71] and it requires payment at one and one-half times an employee's base pay for all hours worked over forty hours in a week.[72]

Compensatory Time Off in Lieu of Payment

If an individual is entitled to payment of overtime under the FLSA, he/she is to receive one and one-half times the hourly rate for all hours worked in excess of forty hours in any one week. An employer can establish any fixed period for the weeks, i.e., Sunday through Saturday, Tuesday through Monday, etc.[73]

The FLSA does not have a provision authorizing compensatory time in lieu of overtime for private employers as each work week stands alone.[74]

---

71   29 U.S.C. § 201 et seq.

72   29 U.S.C. § 207(a)(1)

73   29 CFR 778.105.

74   29 CFR 778.104.

When an employer fails to pay overtime properly, he/she is liable for back wages, plus an equal amount of liquidated damages.[75]

On the surface, this seems straightforward, but questions always arise as to which employees are covered by the FLSA. The term of art used by the statute is exempt and non-exempt. Exempt employees are individuals who are not covered by the FLSA. Non-exempt employees are those individuals for whom the FLSA applies.

Exemptions

There are only four classifications of exempt employees:[76]

Executive

To qualify for the executive employee exemption, all of the following tests must be met:

1. The employee must be compensated on a <u>salary basis</u> (as defined in the regulations) at a rate not less than $455 per week;

2. The employee's primary duty must be managing the enterprise, or managing a customarily recognized department or subdivision of the enterprise;

3. The employee must customarily and regularly direct the work of at least two or more other full-time employees or their equivalent; and

4. The employee must have the authority to hire or fire other employees, or the employee's suggestions and recommendations as to the hiring, firing, advancement, promotion or any other change of status of other employees must be given particular weight.

---

75   29 U.S.C. § 216(a)

76   29 U.S.C. § 213(a)(1)

Administrative

To qualify for the administrative employee exemption, all of the following tests must be met:

1. The employee must be compensated on a <u>salary basis</u> (as defined in the regulations) at a rate not less than $455 per week;

2. The employee's primary duty must be the performance of office or non-manual work directly related to the management or general business operations of the employer or the employer's customers; and

3. The employee's primary duty includes the exercise of discretion and independent judgment with respect to matters of significance.

Professional

To qualify for the learned professional employee exemption, all of the following tests must be met:

1. The employee must be compensated on a <u>salary</u> or fee basis (as defined in the regulations) at a rate not less than $455 per week;

2. The employee's primary duty must be the performance of work requiring advanced knowledge, defined as work which is predominantly intellectual in character and which includes work requiring the consistent exercise of discretion and judgment;

3. The advanced knowledge must be in a field of science or learning and the advanced knowledge must be customarily acquired by a prolonged course of specialized intellectual instruction.

To qualify for the creative professional employee exemption, all of the following tests must be met:

1. The employee must be compensated on a <u>salary</u> or fee basis (as defined in the regulations) at a rate not less than $455 per week;

2. The employee's primary duty must be the performance of work requiring invention, imagination, originality or talent in a recognized field of artistic or creative endeavor.

Computer Employee

To qualify for the computer employee exemption, the following tests must be met:

1. The employee must be compensated either on a <u>salary</u> or fee basis (as defined in the regulations) at a rate not less than $455 per week or, if compensated on an hourly basis, at a rate not less than $27.63 an hour;

2. The employee must be employed as a computer systems analyst, computer programmer, software engineer or other similarly skilled worker in the computer field performing the duties described below;

3. The employee's primary duty must consist of:

    a) The application of systems analysis techniques and procedures, including consulting with users, to determine hardware, software or system functional specifications;

    b) The design, development, documentation, analysis, creation, testing or modification of computer systems or programs, including prototypes, based on and related to user or system design specifications;

    c) The design, documentation, testing, creation or modification of computer programs related to machine operating systems; or

    d) A combination of the aforementioned duties, the performance of which requires the same level of skills.

Outside Sales

To qualify for the outside sales employee exemption, all of the following tests must be met:

1. The employee's primary duty must be making sales (as defined in the FLSA), or obtaining orders or contracts for services or for the use of facilities for which a consideration will be paid by the client or customer; and

2. The employee must be customarily and regularly engaged away from the employer's place or places of business.

Highly Compensated Employee

Highly compensated employees performing office or non-manual work and paid total annual compensation of $100,000 or more (which must include at least $455 per week paid on a salary or fee basis) are exempt from the FLSA if they customarily and regularly perform at least one of the duties of an exempt executive, administrative or professional employee identified in the standard tests for exemption.

Applying the Exemption Test

To determine whether an employee is occupying an exempt or non-exempt position, the employer should look first to the employee's job content, then determine whether the individual is paid on a salaried basis.

If a position's job duties do not fit into one of the four exemptions listed above, it is non-exempt and the employee occupying the position must be paid overtime. When the individual is paid on a salaried basis and the job content does not exempt them from the overtime requirement, that employee is non-exempt.

If an executive, administrative, or professional individual fulfills the job content requirement but is paid on an hourly basis, that employee is non-exempt. When the individual is highly-paid (a systems analyst, computer programmer, software engineer or similarly skilled professional), the employee can be paid hourly and still be exempt. Highly-paid is defined as six and one-half times minimum wage.[77]

It should be remembered that it is the position being evaluated, not the individual. If an individual has an advanced degree and normally would be considered a professional employee but he/she is working in a job that is classified as non-exempt by its job content, that individual would be non-exempt and would be entitled to overtime pay. An employer should evaluate each position within the company to determine whether it is exempt or non-exempt.

Time Cards

All non-exempt employees should complete a weekly timecard, whether or not a time clock is utilized. This will create a record of hours worked in the event there becomes a dispute as to whether a particular employee worked more than forty hours during a given week.

Equal Pay for Equal Work

The Equal Pay Act[78] requires all employees within an establishment to be paid equally for equal work. The Act is specifically designed to ensure that female employees doing similar work as male employees are not paid a lower wage.

In the event an employer discovers unequal pay for equal work, meaning that female employees are paid less, a reduction of the wages of the male employees in an attempt to be in compliance with the Act is prohibited.

Jobs being compared must be substantially equal, but do not have to be identical.[79] The comparison of equal work will generally turn on a qual-

---

77   29 C.F.R. § 541.303.

78   129 U.S.C. § 206(d)(1).

79   *Schultz v. Wheaton Glass Co.*, 421 F.2d 259 (3rd Cir. 1970) (cert. denied) 398 U.S. 905 (1970).

ity of effort.[80] However, the effort must be performed in similar working conditions.[81]

There are legitimate reasons for unequal pay for substantially equal jobs, such as: (1) seniority[82]; and (2) merit pay system.[83]

A seniority system need not be a formalized seniority system, i.e., in writing. It can be one which is part of past practice.[84] However, it is recommended that when an employer wants seniority to play a role in establishment of wage rates, promotions, and/or layoffs, such a policy be formalized as discussed previously. Whether a seniority policy is formalized or is based on past practice, it must be applied uniformly[85] in order to comply with the Act.

Any formal or informal merit pay system must be applied uniformly.

In addition to the above, an incentive pay program can create a differential in pay to individuals. Any incentive pay program must give everyone, regardless of sex, the opportunity to earn the same.[86]

---

80   29 C.F.R. § 1620.8

81   *Corning Glass Works v. Brennan*, 417 U.S. 188 (1974).

82   29 U.S.C. § 206(d)(1).

83   29 U.S.C. § 206(d)(1).

84   *EEOC v. Cleveland State University*, 29 F.E.P. 1782 (N.D. Ohio 1982).

85   *Hodgson v. Washington Hospital*, 9 F.E.P. 612 (W.D. Pa. 1971).

86   *Bence v. Detroit Health Corp.*, 712 F.2d 1024 (6th Cir. 1983) (cert. denied) 46 U.S. 1025.

AGE DISCRIMINATION IN EMPLOYMENT (ADEA)

An employer cannot take into account an individual's age[87] when making any employment decision. Employment decisions affecting compensation, terms and conditions or privileges of employment are what the statute contemplates.[88] When making an employment decision, age can not be the determining factor of the action taken.[89]

In order to establish that age was not the determining factor, an employer will be required to show that the employment decision was based on other reasonable factors.[90] While it is possible for age to be a bona fide occupational qualification, it will be narrowly construed.[91] To have a bona fide occupational qualification for age, the requirement must be reasonably necessary to further an overriding public safety issue or similar policy position.[92]

OCCUPATIONAL SAFETY AND HEALTH (OSHA)

Under OSHA[93], it is every employer's obligation to provide a workplace free from any recognized hazards which could cause harm to her/his employees. To this end, the government has promulgated safety rules which apply either to: (1) all employers; (2) certain industries; or (3) certain situations. In some states, the state has been delegated the respon-

---

87   29 U.S.C. § 623(a)(1)(2)&(3); *La Mantagne v. American Convenience Products*, 750 F.2d 1405 (7th Cir. 1984).

88   29 U.S.C. § 623(a)(1).

89   *La Mantagne v. American Convenience Products*, 750 F.2d 1405 (7th Cir. 1984).

90   *Crimm v. Missouri Pacific R.R.*, 750 F.2d 703 (8th Cir. 1984).

91   *Johnson v. Mayor of Baltimore*, 472 U.S. 353 (1985).

92   *Western Airlines, Inc. v. Criswell*, 472 U.S. 400 (1984).

93   29 U.S.C. § 651 et seq.

sibility to enforce the safety regulations. The responsible agency has the right to inspect, at reasonable times, any business to determine if there are any safety violations.

Employers must ensure employees are provided a safe work environment. It is also the employer's responsibility to see that: (1) every employee is aware of the company's safety policy; (2) there is a mechanism in place to discover whether or not employees are complying with the company's safety policy; and (3) those individuals who don't follow safety rules are disciplined. When these steps are followed by an employer it can be a defense to a citation being issued, this is commonly known as the "employee misconduct" defense.

CONSOLIDATED OMNIBUS BUDGET RECONCILIATION ACT (COBRA)

COBRA[94] requires employers to provide the opportunity for employees and covered spouses and dependents, under certain circumstances, to continue coverage under group medical plans after leaving the employer's employment. All employers who have 20 or more employees must comply with COBRA.

Employers must give a qualified individual notice and opportunity to continue their benefits after a qualifying event.[95] A qualifying event is: (1) when an employer terminates his/her employment; (2) when there is a reduction in an employee's hours; (3) when there is a divorce or legal separation; or (4) when a dependent child ceases to be eligible under the plan requirement.[96]

---

94   29 U.S.C. §1161, et seq.

95   29 U.S.C. §1163.

96   Ibid.

When a qualifying event occurs, the employer must give the individual, their spouse and dependents covered by the benefits, notice of their rights.[97]

Failure to give notice in some instances could make employer/plan administrators liable for medical bills incurred during the relevant time period.[98] In addition to the notice required when there is a qualifying event, at the time an individual becomes eligible to participate in a benefit plan, the employee and/or dependents must be given notice.[99]

EMPLOYEE POLYGRAPH PROTECTION

The Employee Polygraph Protection Act makes it unlawful for any employer to require, request or use polygraph results for any purpose in the employer/employee relationship.[100] This also includes taking an adverse position regarding an applicant or employee for refusing to submit to a polygraph test.[101]

WORKERS' ADJUSTMENT AND RETRAINING NOTIFICATION (WARN)

WARN requires employers with 100 or more employees[102] to provide notice to employees 60 days[103] in advance of certain employer actions. Exceptions to the 60 day notice requirement by the company[104] are: (1)

---

97   29 U.S.C. §1166(a)(4).

98   *Phillips v. Riverside, Inc.*, 796 F. Supp. 403 (E.D. Ark. 1992).

99   29 U.S.C. §1166(a)(1).

100   29 U.S.C. §2002(1)(2).

101   29 U.S.C. § 2002(3)(A)(B).

102   29 U.S.C. § 2002(3)(A)(B).

103   29 U.S.C. § 2102(a).

104   29 U.S.C. § 2102(b).

the company is seeking capital or business which, if acquired, would keep the layoff from occurring; (2) unforeseeable business circumstances; or (3) natural disasters.

The employer actions that trigger the need for WARN notices are: (1) plant closure[105]; or (2) mass layoffs.[106] A mass layoff is defined as a lay-off which is not the result of a plant closure and will result in at least 33 percent of the employees at a single site losing employment in a 30 day period.[107]

The notice must be sent to: (1) the employees affected;[108] (2) the union, if employees are represented by a union;[109] (3) the state dislocated workers' unit;[110] and (4) the chief elected official of the geographic area where the layoffs are to take place.[111] There is no specific requirements for content of notice, although a court has indicated that the reason for the change and why the 60 day notice requirement applies should be specific.[112]

It is recommended that the notice contain the location where layoffs will take place, a contact at the company who can provide information, a statement of what is happening, the date of first separation, and what jobs will be effected.

Failure to comply with the WARN requirements exposes the employer to civil action by each aggrieved employee.[113] The employer could be liable

---

105   29 U.S.C. § 2101.

106   Ibid.

107   29 U.S.C. § 2101(3)(A)(B).

108   29 U.S.C. § 2102(a).

109   Ibid.

110   Ibid. created by the Job Training Partnership Act 29 USC §1651, et seq.

111   29 U.S.C. § 2102(a).

112   *Alarcin v. Keller Industries, Inc.* 27 F.3 86 (9th Cir. 1994).

113   29 U.S.C. §2104(a).

for up to 60 days pay plus attorneys fees for each individual who was laid off without notification.[114]

FAMILY MEDICAL LEAVE ACT (FMLA)

Any employer with fifty (50) or more employees working twenty (20) or more calendar weeks in the preceding calendar year[115] must allow its employees twelve (12) work weeks of unpaid leave.[116] The leave must be granted for: (1) care or birth of a son or daughter;[117] (2) placement of son or daughter with employee for adoption or foster care;[118] (3) caring of spouse, son, daughter, parent of employee for serious health condition;[119] or (4) serious health condition of employee.[120]

Employees taking leave under this section are entitled to return to the position they held prior to their leave commencing[121] or an equivalent position.[122]

Failure to comply can lead to monetary damages assessed against the employer.[123]

---

114 29 U.S.C. §2104(a)(2)(B).

115 29 U.S.C. §2611(4)(A).

116 29 U.S.C. §2612(a)(1).

117 29 U.S.C. §2612(a)(1)(A).

118 29 U.S.C. §2612(a)(1)(B).

119 29 U.S.C. §2612(a)(1)(C).

120 29 U.S.C. §2612(a)(1)(D).

121 29 U.S.C. § 2614(a)(1)(A).

122 20 U.S.C. § 2614(a)(1)(B).

123 29 U.S.C. § 26717(a)(1).

DRUG FREE WORKPLACE ACT OF 1988

Any employer doing business with any federal agency must publish a statement that the place of employment is a drug-free area and that the manufacture, distribution, dispensation and possession of a controlled substance is prohibited.[124] The employer is required to establish a drug-free awareness program[125] and impose penalties for violations.[126]

CIVIL RIGHTS

The civil rights statutes ensure equal rights under the law.[127] These laws guarantee that every citizen of the United States has the right to "make and enforce contracts."[128]

Make and enforce contracts has been defined as the making, performance, modification, and termination[129] as well as the enjoyment of all benefits, privileges, terms and conditions[130] of any contract. This includes all forms of racial discrimination as it relates to contracts.[131]

Employees of private employers[132] are covered by this statute, without regard to the number of employees employed. The statute makes clear all persons are entitled to protection.

---

124 41 U.S.C. § 701(a)(1)(A).

125 41 U.S.C. § 701(a)(1)(B).

126 41 U.S.C. § 701(a)(1)(B)(iv).

127 42 U.S.C. § 1981.

128 42 U.S.C. 1981(a).

129 42 U.S.C. § 1981(b).

130 Ibid.

131 *Allen v. City of Chicago*, (N.D. Ill. 1993), 828 F. Supp. 543.

132 *Waters v. Wisconsin Steel Workers of Int'l Harvestor Co.*, (7th Cir. 1970), 427 F.2d 476, cert. denied 91 SCT 137.

EQUAL EMPLOYMENT OPPORTUNITIES (EEO)

Employers cannot refuse to hire, discharge, promote or otherwise change or reclassify an employee or applicant with respect to compensation, terms, conditions, or privileges of employment based upon race, color, sex, religion or national origin.[133]

Religion

The definition of religion, as it relates to the non-discrimination statutes and laws, is defined beyond the traditional definition of religion to include "…moral or ethical beliefs as to what is right and wrong which are sincerely held with the strength of traditional religious views."[134] When an employee alerts his/her employer that he/she has a "religious belief" that falls into the preceding definition, the employer has a duty to reasonably accommodate that employee's belief.[135] In the event the employee proposes an accommodation, the employer must accept the employee's suggestion unless it will cause an undue hardship for the employer.[136]

Race/Color

Race/color defines a minority group within a society, i.e. African American, American Indian, Asian American, etc. The non-discrimination policy of the statutes and laws goes beyond disparate treatment because of race and/or color to include treatment because of cultural and/or physical differences unique to a particular race/color.

---

133 42 U.S.C. §2000e-2(1) and (2).

134 29 C.F.R. §1605.1.

135 *Estate of Thornton v. Caldor, Inc.*, 554 Supp. 548 (E.D. Mich. 1982).

136 *Ansonia Board of Education v. Philbrook*, 479 U.S. 60 (1986).

National Origin

National origin is defined as any member of a national group of persons with common ancestry, heritage, or background.[137]

Sex

An employer needs to be aware of more than just the obvious areas like selection, promotion, pay, etc., which adversely affect women. Sexual discrimination also includes maternity leaves of absence and sexual harassment.

Generally, maternity leaves are treated like any other medical leave; that is, a physician will determine when an individual must leave work and commence the leave and when the individual is released from medical restrictions to return to work. A mandatory maternity leave, which defines the amount of time that someone is on a leave of absence, is not allowed except in some very narrow circumstances.[138] Such situations would be where the pregnancy creates a risk of serious harm to third parties because the employee cannot fully perform her job, or the employee herself is at risk.

With regards to sexual harassment, it can be manifested in two ways: (1) a hostile work environment;[139] and (2) granting or withholding employee pay or benefits based upon the granting or withholding of sexual favors.[140]

---

137 *Sethy v. Alameda County Water Dist.*, 545 F.2d 1157 (9th Cir. 1976).

138 *Levin v. Delta Air Lines*, 730 F.2d 994 (5th Cir. 1984).

139 *Meritor Savings Bank v. Union*, 477 U.S. 57 (1986).

140 *Priest v. Rotary dba Fireside Motel & Coffee Shoppe*, 634 F. Supp. 571 (N.D. Cal. 1986); *King v. Palmer*, 778 F. 2d 878 (D.C. Cir. 1985); and *Tascono v. Numms*, 570 F. Supp. 1197 (D. Del. 1983).

EQUAL OPPORTUNITIES FOR INDIVIDUALS WITH DISABILITIES ACT, AKA THE AMERICAN DISABILITIES ACT (ADA)

ADA[141] prohibits employers from discriminating against individuals with disabilities.

Companies who have 15 or more employees for 20 or more calendar weeks in any current or preceding year are subject to the Act. As a general rule, an employer should assume the law applies if she/he has more than 15 employees. For an employer with a fluctuating work force, the time period in the second half of the rule would be significant.

A disability as defined by the Act is a physical or mental impairment that substantially limits one or more of life's major activities.[142] Any individual with a disability is protected by the Act only if he/she is a qualified person. A qualified person is defined as someone who, with or without a reasonable accommodation, can perform the essential functions of the particular position.[143] When an employer is evaluating whether an individual can function in a position, she/he must identify the essential functions of the position and determine what, if any, accommodations are necessary for the individual to be able to handle the essential functions of the position. As an example, if one of the essential functions of a position is highly technical and requires technical training, and the disabled individual lacks the technical training, the disabled person is not qualified.

A reasonable accommodation under the Act[144] may include: (a) making existing facilities usable; (b) restructuring a particular position; (c) modifying work schedules; and/or (d) the acquisition or modification of equipment. The accommodation should not create an undue hardship on the employer. In determining whether an undue hardship is created for an

---

141   42 U.S.C. § 12101, *et seq.*

142   42 U.S.C. §12102 (5)(a).

143   42 U.S.C. §12111 (8).

144   42 U.S.C. §12111 (9).

employer, consideration is given to: a) the cost of the accommodation; b) financial resources of the facility if the employer has multiple facilities; c) financial resources of the employer; and d) the type of operation and/or the makeup of the work force. In addition, an employer may be required to keep a position open for a qualified disabled individual if that would be a reasonable accommodation.

During the hiring process, an employer cannot inquire of a prospective employee what accommodation may be required for the individual to do the job. Such an inquiry can only be pursued after the hiring decision is made. An individual applicant must be accepted or rejected prior to any discussions of reasonable accommodation. There should be no inquiries into an applicant's medical history.

The employer should develop a job description outlining the essential functions of the position. All individuals should be interviewed uniformly, comparing their experience to requirements in the job descriptions.

When there is an on-the-job injury involving a current employee, the injury itself will fall within the scope of each state's Worker's Compensation Statutes. However, ADA may well govern the individual's return to work. ADA obligations requiring reasonable accommodation will be required in such circumstances.

A violation of ADA will occur if an employer becomes aware of a disability as described in the ADA and takes any adverse action against the individual based upon the disability.

EVALUATING PERFORMANCE

After an employee is hired, the previously discussed position description will be useful to objectively monitor performance. Evaluating an individual's performance in their position allows for 360-degree feedback. The employer can explain to the employee what is expected and how the individual is performing against expectations and it gives the employee the opportunity to discuss his/her career development. The employer should select comfortable performance review intervals; keeping in mind that when the policy is established, the employer must be consistent in following through with the process. Generally, the intervals used are: 1) after the first six months, then annually for exempt employees, or 2) after three months, then annually for nonexempt employees. The fact that the evaluating process takes place is what is important, not the timing of the intervals,.

The appraisal form itself may be anything from a document that requires considerable written explanation to a simple check the appropriate box. Once again the form isn't what is important, completing the form is what is important.

See Appendix F a sample performance appraisal.

EMPLOYEE DISCIPLINE

Although most states are governed by employment-at-will, a progressive discipline approach to handling problems with employees can be helpful, first by giving the employer a contemporaneous documented record of an individual's work history in the event of litigation, and secondly, and more importantly, by perhaps turning a less than satisfactory employee into a satisfactory employee. *See* Appendix D. An employer must keep in mind that when a policy such as this is adopted, it becomes an exception to the employment-at-will doctrine and must be followed consistently. A progressive discipline system would involve multiple steps.[145] 1) documented oral performance counseling; 2) written counseling statement; 3) formal investigation/personal development plan; and 4) termination. Should this procedure be outlined in the employee handbook and not be followed, the individual cannot be terminated without exposure to a claim of wrongful termination. The policy should also state that for a serious offense, an individual can be terminated without warning.

---

145 *Guadian Industries Corp.,* 319 NLRB 74 (1995).

The NLRB has established that an employee may have another employee present when an employer counsels an employee on work-related issues. This is a common practice in a union environment, but now must be followed in a non-union environment as well.[146]

TERMINATION

There may come a time when an employer and employee separate. If this is to be a separation for lack of work, it is important that a policy for reducing staff for economic conditions be developed before it is needed (refer to employee handbook/company policies).

In the event that the separation from employment is due to performance issues, it is recommended that no decision be made without quiet reflection. It is strongly recommended that the situation be reviewed and evaluated calmly. An employer must be sure the basis for the termination is articulated to the individual and copied to the individual's file. This must be the real reason and must be non-discriminatory and defensible. To assist in this, a guideline for making such decisions is outlined at Appendix G.

RECORD KEEPING REQUIREMENTS

The records generated from the Employer/Employee relationship, such as applications, evaluations and all other documents have legal requirements regarding how long they must be maintained by an employer.[147]

Employers must maintain certain records relating to any employee action for a period of one year from the date of its creation or the action described in the record, whichever is longer.

---

146 *NLRB v. Epilepsy Foundation of NE Ohio*, 331 NLRB 92 (2000).

147 ERISA, note 19; FLSA, note 67; ADEA, note 83; OSHA, note 89; WARN, note 98; FMLA, note 111; EEO, note 129.

In addition, records containing an employee's: (1) name; (2) address; (3) date of birth; (4) occupation; (5) rate of pay; and (6) weekly compensation must be maintained for three years. ERISA requires records to be kept for a period of six years.

Applications, promotion records, physical examination results, benefit and pension records must be kept for one year. See appendix E for more detail.

CONCLUSION

The Human Resource Management function as a part of an employer's role is challenging but can also be rewarding. As shown, there are no insignificant details in the employer's role of interacting with its employees. What may seem a simple task of filling a position with a qualified individual becomes much more involved when the employer must maintain compliance with the laws, insure the individual hired is compensated properly, and, if necessary, disciplined fairly. This applies to every facet of dealing with employees.

A caring, involved employer is vital to any organization's survival.

APPENDIX A
POSITION DESCRIPTION

TITLE _____   Salary Grade_____

Name of Immediate Supervisor_____   Approval_____

Number of Immediate Subordinates_____   Approval Date_____

Position is:___ Exempt ___ Non-Exempt[148] Revision Date _____

GENERAL SUMMARY

ESSENTIAL FUNCTIONS

SCOPE OF RESPONSIBILITY

SPECIFIC SKILLS REQUIRED

EDUCATION AND EXPERIENCE REQUIRED

GENERAL WORKING CONDITIONS

The categories contained in this job description are not necessarily all-inclusive; additional duties may be assigned and requirements may vary from time to time.

---

148 *See* discussion of exempt/non-exempt under Fair Labor and Standards Act.

APPENDIX B
EMPLOYMENT APPLICATION

PLEASE PRINT LEGIBLY   DATE: _____

NAME_____
            Last   First   Middle

ADDRESS _____ CITY _____ ZIP _____

PHONE (__)_____MESSAGE PHONE (IF DIFFERENT)(__)_____

SOCIAL SECURITY NO. _____DRIVER'S LIC. # _____

ARE YOU UNDER 18? ____POSITION APPLYING FOR_____

BEGINNING SALARY EXPECTED: __ DATE AVAILABLE TO START _____

PLEASE LIST THE DAYS AND TIMES YOU COULD NORMALLY WORK

     SUN____MON___TUES___WED___THUR__FRI____SAT

EMPLOYMENT HISTORY

PLEASE BEGIN WITH LAST EMPLOYER FIRST, ATTACH ADDITIONAL SHEET IF NEEDED

NAME OF EMPLOYER_____

FIRST POSITION HELD _____LAST POSITION HELD _____

DATE BEGAN _____DATE ENDED _____

BEGINNING RATE OF PAY_____ENDING RATE OF PAY _____

REASON FOR LEAVING _____

IMMEDIATE EMPLOYER _____PHONE NO. _____

EDUCATION

TRADE OR VOCATIONAL SCHOOL _____

COURSE OF STUDY _____

LOCATION _____DATE COMPLETED_____

COLLEGE OR UNIVERSITY_____

COURSE OF STUDY _____

LOCATION DATE COMPLETED _____

HIGH SCHOOL OR EQUIVALENCY_____

LOCATION _____DATE COMPLETED_____

PERSONAL REFERENCES

PLEASE LIST THREE PEOPLE WHO HAVE KNOWN YOU IN A NON-PROFESSIONAL CAPACITY FOR A MINIMUM OF TWO YEARS AND A PHONE NUMBER FOR EACH.

NAME_____ PHONE_____

NAME_____ PHONE_____

NAME_____ PHONE_____

HAVE YOU EVER APPLIED FOR EMPLOYMENT OR BEEN EMPLOYED HERE BEFORE? _____
IF SO, WHEN? _____

ARE YOU LEGALLY ELIGIBLE TO WORK IN THE U.S.?_____

TYPE OF VISA HELD _____

ARE YOU OVER THE AGE OF 18? _____ YES   _____ NO

HAVE YOU EVER BEEN CONVICTED OF A FELONY? _____

IF YES, PLEASE LIST DETAILS _____

_____

WOULD YOU BE WILLING TO TRANSFER LOCATIONS WITHIN THE COMPANY? _____

The information provided in this application is true and accurate.

_____

Signature of Applicant

COMPLETION OF THIS APPLICATION
DOES NOT CONSTITUTE AN OFFER OF EMPLOYMENT
EQUAL OPPORTUNITY EMPLOYER M/F

APPENDIX C
POSTER REQUIREMENTS

These notices pertain to federal statutes only. Most states have additional notice requirements. Employers should check with their particular state's agencies to determine the requirements for their respective state.

Poster Identity	Basic Requirements	To Obtain Poster
Equal Employment Opportunity is the Law Vietnam Era Veteran's Readjustment Assistance Act of 1974, as amended.	Prohibits job discrimination based on race, color, religion, sex or national origin; also anti-bias laws protecting handicapped persons and veterans.	Equal Employment Opportunity Commission Washington, D.C. 20506
Notice to Employees Working on Federal or Federally Financed Construction Projects.	Establishes minimum hourly rate and 1½ for hours after 40 hours per week; also covers equal pay and child labor.	U.S. Department of Labor Wage and Hour Division Washington, D.C. 20210
Notice to Employees Working on Government Contracts.	Contractors and subcontractors engaged in federal service contracts exceeding $2500 must post minimum wage and benefits required per the contract.	U.S. Department of Labor Wage and Hour Division Washington, D.C. 20210

Poster Identity	Basic Requirements	To Obtain Poster
Job Safety and Health Protection (OSHA).	Requires employers furnish employees a place free from recognized hazards that might cause serious injury or death. Employees must comply with safety and health standards, rules, etc.	U.S. Department of Labor, OSHA OSHA Publication 37535 Washington, D.C. 20013-7535
Notice: Employee Polygraph Protection Act.	Prohibits private employers from utilizing lie detector tests in pre-employment screening and during employment. States exceptions (government, national security).	U.S. Department of Labor Employment Standards Administration Wage and Hour Division Washington, D.C. 20210
Notice to Workers with Disabilities Paid at Special Minimum Wage.	Satisfies requirement when Employer has Workers working under special minimum wage certificates.	Equal Employment Opportunity Commission Public Affairs Office 2401 E Street NW Room 4056 Washington, D.C. 20506
Federal Minimum Wage Employment Standards Under the Fair Labor Standards Act.	Establishes Federal minimum wage.	U.S. Department of Labor Employment Standards Division Wage and Hour Division Washington, D.C. 20210

Poster Identity	Basic Requirements	To Obtain Poster
Your Rights Under the Family and Medical Leave Act.	Establishes 12 weeks of unpaid, job protected leave to "eligible" employees for certain family and medical reasons.	U.S. Department of Labor Employment Standards Division Wage and Hour Division Washington, D.C. 20210
Notice Migrant and Seasonal Agricultural Worker Protection Act.	Explains the rights and protections for migrant workers.	U.S. Department of Labor Employment Standards Division Wage and Hour Division Washington, D.C. 20210
Uniformed Services Employment and Reemployment rights act.	Covers the requirements of employers to rehire employees returning form the uniformed service.	Equal Employment Opportunity Commission Washington, D.C. 20506

APPENDIX D
COMPANY POLICIES

While this list covers a number of areas, it is not exhaustive. The employer should not assume it is a comprehensive list for an employee handbook, but should design an employee handbook to fit the unique situation of the particular employer.

Policy	Why	Proposed
Probation Period	A period during which employer and employee evaluate one another. Benefits generally commence at end of probation period. Employer can terminate employee without progressive discipline.	Probation can be a time of 30-60-90 days. Generally not longer than 90 days although some companies have used 180 days.
Holidays	Establish those days which company will give paid time off. There could be unpaid holidays, this is at the employer's discretion.	Companies generally give the traditional days for holidays (New Years, President's Day, Memorial Day, 4th of July, Labor Day, Thanksgiving and Christmas), but a company can give as many or few as desired. The employee may be required to work the day before and after the holiday to be eligible to receive pay.

Policy	Why	Proposed
Sick Leave	Paid time employees can use if they are sick, for doctor's appointments, etc.	Generally, accrued at the rate of one day per month, but this is at the employer's discretion. Employer may require doctor's certificate to receive pay. Employee may bank up to maximum number of days. Employer may or may not pay upon separation from company.
Vacation	Establishes paid time off for employees.	Vacation can be established at whatever the employer deems fair. Generally the longer an employee works, the more vacation is earned. Employers should reserve right of scheduling vacation time off. Employer must pay unused earned vacation at time of separation.
Leave of Absence	Establishes unpaid time off during which length of service is not broken.	Leaves of absence are generally for: personal; education; medical; maternity; paternity; or military reasons. Leaves of absence must be administered without regard to race, sex, or age. Medical, maternity, paternity and military leaves require employer to bring employee back to job and pay as if the individual had never left the company.

Policy	Why	Proposed
Work Rules	Establishes dos and don'ts in the work place.	Work rules should be tied into the disciplinary policy and a severe breach, such as jeopardizing safety of others, could result in immediate termination.
Disciplinary Action	Establishes system of discipline to ensure consistent action throughout company.	Discipline is generally progressive: (1) verbal warning; (2) written warning; (3) performance improvement plan; (4) termination.
Termination	Establishes who in company has authority to terminate an employee.	Terminations must be handled in such a way as to ensure race, sex, age, national origin is not the basis for the action.
Safety	A safe work environment is required by OSHA.	A written safety program should be developed; depending on type of business, a lifting program may be needed.
Jury Duty	Employer must give employees time off if called to serve on jury duty.	Whether an employee receives regular pay is discretionary with employer.
Wage Garnishment	Establishes how to handle garnishments of employee wages when received. If employer doesn't respond in timely fashion, it could be liable for full amount of employee's debt.	Employee can not be terminated for multiple garnishments on single debt.

Policy	Why	Proposed
Hazardous Material Disclosure	Employees have right to know materials they are working around.	Materials must be labeled; first aid must be available.
Patents, Copyrights of Employees	Employers need to ensure that when employees use company time, assets, knowledge, etc. to create something, that ownership remains with the employer.	Such a policy must comply with each state's statute.
Promotions	Establishes system for identifying and promoting individuals to ensure there is no discrimination based on sex, age, race, national origin, etc.	Promotions program may be straight seniority, posting of jobs or that which fits employers work environment, but discrimination must not exist.
Sexual Harassment	Employer must establish policy that sexual harassment will not be tolerated by its company and/or employees.	An anti-sexual harassment statement should be included.
Solicitation	Employer should establish by whom, when and where employees may be solicited by non-employees and employees.	Non-employees should not be allowed to solicit employees on company premises. Employees should not be allowed to solicit employees on work time.

Policy	Why	Proposed
Vendor Anti-Discrimination	Employer should require outside vendors to sign statement of non-discrimination. This is required of government contractors.	A short statement sent to the vendor should be sufficient.
Equal Employment Opportunity	Employer should establish overall policy against discrimination based on age, sex, race, national origin, etc.	If employer is government contractor, an affirmative action plan could be required.
Reference for Former Employees	Employer should establish policy for handling calls checking references of former employees.	Employer should only verify information caller has, not volunteer additional information.
Attendance	Employer will be able to deal with employees consistently regarding absenteeism.	Establish procedure to excuse absence and call-in for employees when they will not be coming to work.
E-Mail	Company will minimize potential liability that can result from monitoring E-mail.	Establish a policy that places employees on notice that E-mail may be monitored.
Tardiness	Employer will be able to deal with employees consistently regarding tardiness.	Establish call-in procedure to deal with excessive tardiness. Define what excessive is.
Drug Free Work Place	Establishes that work place is drug free zone.	Use, manufacturing, sale, etc. of drugs is improper. Basis for disciplinary action.

APPENDIX E
FEDERAL STATUTES

CHAPTER	TITLE/DESCRIPTION	SIZE OF EMPLOYER & RECORD RETENTION REQUIRMENTS
29 USC §100 et seq.	EMPLOYMENT RETIREMENT INCOME SECURITY ACT (ERISA)	All Employers must maintain ERISA-related records for a minimum of six years.
29 USC §141 et seq.	NATIONAL LABOR RELATIONS ACT (NLRA)	All
29 USC §201 et seq.	FEDERAL FAIR LABOR STANDARDS ACT (FLSA) EQUAL PAY ACT	All For at least three years.
29 USC § 621 et seq.	AGE DISCRIMINATION IN EMPLOYMENT (ADEA)	All Three years for payroll or other records showing basic employee information. One year for applications and other personnel records. Where a charge or lawsuit is filed, all relevant records must be kept until "final disposition" of the charge or lawsuit.

CHAPTER	TITLE/DESCRIPTION	SIZE OF EMPLOYER & RECORD RETENTION REQUIRMENTS
29 USC §651 et seq.	OCCUPATIONAL SAFETY AND HEALTH (OSHA)	All Five years. Injury reports Employee's job tenure plus thirty years.
29 USC §1161 et seq.	CONSOLIDATED OMNIBUS BUDGET RECONCILIATION ACT (COBRA)	20 or more employees
29 USC §2001 et seq.	EMPLOYEE POLYGRAPH PROTECTION	All Three years.
29 USC §2101	WORKER ADJUSTMENT AND RETRAINING NOTIFICATION (WARN)	100 or more employees
29 USC §2601 et seq.	FAMILY MEDICAL LEAVE ACT (FMLA)	50 or more employees Three years.
41 USC §701 et seq.	DRUG-FREE WORKPLACE ACT OF 1988	Government contractors
42 USC §1981 et seq.	CIVIL RIGHTS	All

CHAPTER	TITLE/DESCRIPTION	SIZE OF EMPLOYER & RECORD RETENTION REQUIRMENTS
42 USC §2000e	EQUAL EMPLOYMENT OPPORTUNITIES (EEO)	15 or more employees * Note: Compensatory damages are limited according to size of employer see 42 USC 1981(a) One year from making the record or taking the personnel action. Where a charge or lawsuit is filed, all relevant records must be kept until "final disposition." A copy of the current EEO-1 Report must be retained.
42 USC §12101 et seq.	AMERICANS WITH DISABILITIES ACT (ADA)	15 or more employees One year from making the record or taking the personnel action. Where a charge or lawsuit is filed, all relevant records must be kept until "final disposition."

APPENDIX F
PERFORMANCE EVALUATION

Employee _____   Date of Hire _____

Evaluator _____   Date of Evaluation _____

Reviewed by _____

<u>Factors Being Evaluated</u>   <u>Levels of Performance</u>

	Unsat.*	Good	Very good	Outstanding*
• Job knowledge	☐	☐	☐	☐
• Quality of work	☐	☐	☐	☐
• Quantity of work	☐	☐	☐	☐
• Promptness in completing assignment	☐	☐	☐	☐
• Judgment	☐	☐	☐	☐
• Initiative shown	☐	☐	☐	☐
• Ingenuity shown	☐	☐	☐	☐
• Acceptance of responsibility	☐	☐	☐	☐
• Ability to get along with others	☐	☐	☐	☐
• Attitude	☐	☐	☐	☐
• Attendance and promptness	☐	☐	☐	☐

* For any response of Unsatisfactory or Outstanding, please elaborate here.

_____

Please explain employee's:

Strengths _____

Weaknesses _____

Accomplishments against previously set goals_____

_____

Goals for next evaluation period _____

_____

_____ [employee's signature]

_____ [employer's signature]

DEFINITIONS

1. <u>Unsatisfactory</u>: Performance meets minimum acceptable standards in most instances, but is unsatisfactory in some cases; improvement is necessary. Assignments are occasionally submitted late and/or are incomplete. Detailed direction and frequent progress checks are usually required. The employee is normally in a learning phase or of questionable ability to meet job requirements.

2. <u>Good</u>: Performance of most duties is adequate, meets most standards in an acceptable manner. Some improvement may be necessary. Occasionally may fail to complete assignments on time and/or comprehensively. Requires direction and review of major parts of assignments. May hesitate to undertake work outside his/her defined area of responsibility. Understands most duties and overall objectives of the job. The employee is beyond the learning phase and is making measurable contributions within limited areas.

3. <u>Very Good</u>: Performs all duties and responsibilities in a comprehensive manner. Little need for improvement to be considered fully adequate for the job. Infrequently may not complete specific assignments on schedule. Generally works independently. Requires infrequent progress reviews. Handles assignments in a professional manner and seeks out work in a related area. Makes contributions to the overall effectiveness of the department or terminal.

4. <u>Outstanding</u>: Performs all duties and responsibilities in a thoroughly comprehensive manner. Some duties are carried out in a superior manner. Efficiently uses time, manpower, and funds in carrying out assignments. Considered highly knowledgeable by superiors, peers, and subordinates. Sought out for advice and assistance, consistently makes significant contributions to the overall effectiveness of the department or terminal.

APPENDIX G
GUIDELINE TO EMPLOYEE SEPARATION

The following is intended to be used as a guide to follow when making the decision to separate an employee from employment. Most questions ask for a "Yes" or "No" response. If the answer is No to any question, or if it is difficult to answer Yes, the decision to separate the employee should be re-evaluated.

WHAT IS THE REASON FOR THIS TERMINATION?

[ ]	Unsatisfactory Performance	GO TO I.
[ ]	Violation of Company Rule(s)	GO TO II.
[ ]	Other Misconduct or Infraction	GO TO III.
[ ]	Insubordination	GO TO IV.

I. UNSATISFACTORY PERFORMANCE

A. Performance Evaluations

__Yes __No 1. Have formal performance evaluations and/or appraisals been completed on a regular basis?

__Yes __No 2. Have the performance deficiencies leading to this decision to separate this employee been cited in the most recent of the performance evaluations?

__Yes __No 3. Are the performance standards cited as deficient "job-related," i.e., are they necessary and/or important to the successful completion of this employee's job?

__Yes __No 4. Has the employee acknowledged and/or been provided a copy of past evaluations, indicating an acknowledgment or awareness of these deficiencies?

__Yes __No   5.   Is the situation leading up to this separation decision reflected in this employee's personnel file?

              6.   Continue to Section B.

        B.   Performance Deficiencies

__Yes __No   1.   Can it be concluded the employee was given advance notice specifying the requirements of the job, and the standards by which job performance would be judged?

__Yes __No   2.   In the event there are no formal evaluations, was the employee given notice of his/her job performance deficiencies?

__Yes __No   3.   Was this employee given assistance and/or counseling to assist in rectifying performance deficiencies?

__Yes __No   4.   Was the employee given a reasonable time period and/or opportunity to correct these deficiencies?

              5.   Go to section V.

II.   VIOLATION OF COMPANY RULES

        A.   Establishment of Work Rules

__Yes __No   1.   Is the rule violated necessary and reasonably related to the safe and/or efficient operation of the company?

__Yes __No   2.   Does the rule concern only work-related conduct?

__Yes __No   3.   Is the rule written in a clear and understandable manner?

             4.   Continue to section B.

       B.   <u>Employee Notice of Rules</u>

__Yes __No   1.   Have the work rules been disseminated to all employees?

__Yes __No   2.   Can it be established that this employee has received notice of the work rules generally, and/or the particular work rule involved here?

             3.   Continue to section III.

III.   <u>**MISCONDUCT AND OTHER INFRACTIONS**</u>

       A.   <u>Notice of Violation</u>

__Yes __No   1.   If this is not a violation of a written rule, would the average employee be expected to understand that his/her action would constitute misconduct in the company's view?

__Yes __No   2.   Has the employee been given notice previously of his/her misconduct or infraction?

__Yes __No   3.   Was the employee given a reasonable opportunity to take constructive corrective action?

             4.   Continue to section B.

B.   Pre-Termination Investigation

__Yes __No   1.   Was a fair, prompt, and thorough investigation conducted?

__Yes __No   2.   Was the investigation conducted prior to making the decision to separate this employee?

__Yes __No   3.   Was the employee given a complete opportunity to give his/her side of the story?

__Yes __No   4.   Have company procedures been followed? Specifically, has the employee received the requisite number and types of warnings pursuant to the company procedure regarding progressive discipline?

__Yes __No   5.   If the employee is covered by a collective bargaining agreement, have all contractual procedures followed?

__Yes __No   6.   If the employee is covered by a collective bargaining agreement, was he/she afforded the opportunity to union representation if requested?

7.   Go to section V.

IV.   **INSUBORDINATION**

__Yes __No   1.   Was the employee given a clear and direct order, which he/she understood or reasonably should have understood?

__Yes __No   2.   Was the order given by someone the employee would or should have known to have the authority to issue such an order?

__Yes __No   3.   Was the order reasonably related to the employee's job?

__Yes __No   4.   Was the employee forewarned that refusal to obey the order would or could result in termination?

5.   Go to section V.

V.   <u>FINAL CONSIDERATIONS BEFORE SEPARATION</u>

__Yes __No   1.   Is the violation serious enough to warrant the firing of this employee?

__Yes __No   2.   Is this decision consistent with actions taken in cases in the past?

__Yes __No   3.   Are there any mitigating factors or extenuating circumstances which would justify some other disciplinary action?

__Yes __No   4.   Is this decision timely? (i.e., within a reasonable period of time following the violation or was there a reasonable period of time afforded to correct unsatisfactory performance?)

__Yes __No   5.   Does the entire record support the decision?

__Yes __No   6.   Is there a good documented record, in the event the decision is challenged?

__Yes __No   7.   Has there been a reasonable attempt to accommodate this individual situation?

__Yes __No   8.   Does the Company's employee handbook and/or policy manual contain language establishing that employment is "at-will," and that there are no guarantees or promises of continued employment?

9.   **Finally, is this decision based on reason(s) other than:**

   a.   Age
   b.   Race, color, national origin
   c.   Sex
   d.   Religion
   e.   Handicap
   f.   Marital status
   g.   Military status
   h.   Reporting a safety or health violation (OSHA/WISHA)
   i.   Refusing to participate in an unlawful activity
   j.   Reporting any unlawful activity
   k.   To avoid vesting in a pension plan
   l.   Union activity, including filing grievances

If the answer to all of these questions is Yes, the decision to separate this employee is well-founded and should withstand scrutiny by any reviewing regulatory agency, court, or grievance arbitrator. If, on the other hand, the answer to one or more areas is No, there is a potential for problems.

978-0-595-38756-4
0-595-38756-X